Exclamation Mark of Tears

EXCLAMATION MARK OF TEARS

Resource Publications
An Imprint of Wipf and Stock Publishers
199 W. 8th Ave., Suite 3
Eugene, OR 97401

www.wipfandstock.com

PAPERBACK ISBN: 979-8-3852-7327-0
HARDCOVER ISBN: 979-8-3852-7328-7
EBOOK ISBN: 979-8-3852-7329-4

Exclamation Mark of Tears

WANSOO KIM

Foreword by Dustin Pickering

RESOURCE *Publications* • Eugene, Oregon

Contents

Foreword: Exclamation Mark of Tears: Healing of Our Divisions

BY DUSTIN PICKERING, A POET AND CRITIC IN TEXAS, USA

WE ARE LIVING IN contentious times. In such times, the power of poetry to bridge cultures and instill dialogue is without question. Poets don't shy away from politically heated topics. Coleridge believed in pantisocracy, an idea stemming from the French Revolution where "liberty, equality, fraternity" were the ideals. Pantisocracy is a utopian and egalitarian belief in a government by all where duties and resources are mutually shared. Some 20th century poets such as Carl Sandburg were also politically idealistic, viewing socialism as the answer to the human dilemma. Even conservative poets like Eliot saw the fragmentation created by war and impoverished morality in his long poem "The Wasteland." Ideals guide poetry and art, and art reflects the human condition, serving as a mirror back to the individual soul.

Wansoo Kim in *Exclamation Mark of Tears* reflects the grief and shared pain of the human condition throughout contemporary global unrest and uncertainty. The title itself expresses urgency and pain. In this four-part collection, Kim bandages the wounds of the world inflicted by wars, poverty, climate crises, confusion of values, and catastrophe. Poetry is a medium toward understanding the world and offering reconciliation with it. Shelley wrote, "Poetry lifts the veil from the hidden beauty of the world, and makes familiar objects be as if they were not familiar." His period was also full of unrest as urbanization and rapid industrialization were leaving many without basic human rights. Blake wrote of the problems facing the poor and needy as well in poems such as "The Chimney Sweeper," a poem reflecting not only the pain but the dreams of needy children in 18th-century England.

Kim writes in the preface, "I wrote this collection of poems to reflect on these global crises and to urge people around the world to join in reflection and action, using the image of tears, rich in symbolic meaning." The purpose of this collection is to encourage "reflection and action" to mitigate the problems the world faces. Kim advises readers to "come together in prayer and cooperation." His eloquent words serve as a medium to encourage readers and uplift through a shared pain.

For instance, he evokes John Donne in the lines, "I do not know for whom the bell tolls— / But the bells of war tear through all our hearts." These two lines remind us of death's anonymity in places torn by war and conflict such as Sudan, Gaza, and Ukraine. While people on both sides of a conflict suffer and countries are ripped asunder spiritually, the bells of war "tear through all our hearts." The fear of conflict divides even those who are spiritually awake, and since both sides hope their sense of justice and outcry will be acknowledged, war inevitably breeds division.

In "For Whom Does the Bell Ring?" Kim writes these lines:

> "In the ruins of a hospital, bloodied scalpels lie still,
> A white coat sowing cries into the empty air."

This opening poem reminds us that even healers require the patience of healing. War's traumas leave us all powerless.

In the next poem "The Silent Gods" the poet writes: "Like flocks of migratory birds, bombers swoop, / Missiles plunge toward Palestine like meteors, / And Israel's boiling blood turns into blazing flames, / Swallowing the ancient land. / A Palestinian girl stands dazed before her shattered home." The use of natural imagery to describe war's brutality serves a dual purpose of suggesting humankind's power resembles that of the natural world, and also encompasses Shelley's previously quoted statement that poetry "lifts the veil." Even in horrific times, beauty can still maintain its purpose. Kim further writes:

> "Fragile lives wither like flower petals,
> The names of gods scatter as black ash,
> The sky is stained crimson, the earth turns to hell."

The gods are silent, yet they still exist within the fragility of life. Through this fragility, the poem reveals that the way we view the world reflects what we truly value. The final question—"Have humans left the embrace of the gods?"—asks whether we have abandoned not only the gods themselves, but also the values they represent.

Kim's stark imagery, recurring throughout the collection, reflects a deeply moral worldview. In "Poets, Let Us Rise Together," he calls on his fellow poets to foster solidarity within the literary community.

> "Poets,
> Let us lift the lantern of wisdom.
> Though we cannot completely hush evil's whisper,
> We can send poems to shine the path with a merciful light"

While the poet realizes poetry cannot rid the world of its moral dilemma, it offers "merciful light."

The poems embrace unity and hope rather than horror and hate. Kim carefully chooses metaphors to remind readers of the promise children offer. In "Cry for North Korea 2" these lines resonate:

> "People of the South, shed your tears,
> Don't you hear the silent cry
> Of starving brothers?
> Longing still breathes—
> Let us join hands and pray
> For children's laughter to bloom
> In North and South alike."

As a South Korean, Wansoo Kim reminds his country to consider the sorrow of hunger in their neighboring country. The embrace of "children's laughter" and prayer offers solidarity for all Koreans.

The poem following is dedicated to South Korea. Kim writes:

> "O leader of the North,
> If your heart still stirs,
> Bring forth the dusty smile of childhood
> And reveal the soul stained with tears."

These lines appeal to the North Korean leadership through shared humanity and love for the gentler things in life. The poem is a reminder that an appeal can be made even unto the darkest shadows of the human soul.

In "The River of Waiting" the poet turns the world vision to himself:

> "Even when I'm irritated or weary,
> I will lay down the sharp stones aimed at you
> And hide the fire-lit or ice-cold glint in my eyes.
> Even beneath the dust of all the passing time,
> I won't turn away or give you my back—
> I'll quietly wait like a mother by the window."

These personal lines share with the reader's impatience to remind us of Kim's moral vision. In a world fraught with longing for peace during intense conflict and destruction, impatience might be our most embraced vice. Impatience is divisive. Sitting quietly in a world of distractions is perhaps the best medicine.

The poet's humane moral vision extends to the natural world. In "Tears of the Sea" Kim humanizes the pain of the sea.

> "The sea rides on rough waves,
> And in the suffocating stench,
> It cries out like a dying breath—
> "Black water scales are spreading all over my body,
> My once-blue breath has grown thin, about to break."

The symbolization of death reflects desperation and fear. Kim's imagery and symbolization provide an analogy to the human world in order to appeal to readers' humane sense. The urgency expressed in the poet's language is conveyed to the readership which may take nature for granted.

In "The Digital Sea" the analogy takes the reverse route. Kim writes, "Gales, thick with deceitful dust, / Churn the sea without rest, / And even the roots of once-green trees are shaken." This metaphor reflects the impatience of digital distraction. By appealing metaphorically to natural images, the poet liberates the imagination from digital distraction.

The third section of the poetry collection explores the theme of 'values.' In "In Light Shining in the Darkness," the poem reveals the diversity and significance of values through various forms of devotion:

"Some pave the path with sweat and tears, / While others set themselves ablaze, / Burying a star of hope within the darkness of the world." Capturing the diverse aspects of sacrifice and devotion, these lines remind readers of the power of labor to sustain hope and create a new world. Persistence is a virtue that demands "sweat and tears," while life itself is portrayed as the "star of hope within the darkness of the world." In "Master of Life" the star again makes an appearance:

> "When a sudden whirlwind strikes
> And shadows like black beasts stain the soul,
> A single starlight deep within me whispers:
> "Like the deep and silent night sky,
> Embrace stillness even in the midst of chaos.
> That light shining through your darkness
> Is an invisible thread binding us together."

The invisible thread may be interpreted as a transcendent presence or inner conscience that binds humanity together in compassion. Kim's parallel use of images gives the collection its unified vision.

In "Trees of the Soul" the poet clarifies his moral vision of ethical contribution. "Like a red flower blooming in the family garden, / As gripping pain and cold sweat spread across the chest, / When the cry of new life bursts forth, / Joy and tears bloom together" This implies that hope blossoms from pain, much like a new sprout needs hardship as nourishment to grow. Kim writes, asserting the value of persistence.

Later poems such as "The Queer Festival in Korea" suggest a broader sense of human dignity.

> "Beneath the rainbow-colored flag,
> Tears of light and shadow flow over dancing souls.
> Rain falls from the sky like a heartfelt prayer,
> Soaking the parched, cracked earth as if by healing hands,
> And it sprouts new shoots."

In "Korea's Queer Festival," poet Kim writes, "Beneath the rainbow-colored flag / tears mixed with light and shadow flow over the dancing souls." In this line, the "tears mixed with light and shadow" go beyond mere emotional expression; they encapsulate the complexity of a reality where both discrimination and welcome coexist. The following image—"rainfall descending like an earnest prayer from the heavens"—portrays rain as a spiritual conduit between sky and humanity. As it moistens the parched earth, it symbolically suggests the healing and regeneration of marginalized lives. Here, rain functions not just as a natural phenomenon but as a metaphorical device enabling social renewal and inclusion. Through such imagery, Kim poetically implies that embracing diversity is the true path to harmony. In this way, the natural images in his poetry are not mere ornamentation but serve as a living language that conveys ethical messages.

In "Love That Keeps the Ember Alive," a fitting closure to the collection, Kim returns to the image of collective responsibility:

> "When we hand over a warm bowl of soup,
> Gently hold a dry hand,
> Listen to the lonely one's story,
> Love quietly takes root
> And will become someone's ember."

Exclamation Mark of Tears offers a sincere moral vision informed not by dogma but by a spiritual longing for wholeness.

The defining features of Wansoo Kim's poetic craft are his seamless integration of classical literary techniques—such as apostrophe, rhetorical repetition(including anaphora), and extended metaphor—with a contemporary global consciousness. His use of personification, particularly in poems like "Tears of the Sea" and "The Tears of the Glacier," brings nature to life not just as setting but as suffering subject, echoing a prophetic voice. Kim also frequently employs enjambment and internal rhythmic patterns that subtly underscore the emotional undercurrents of his lines without overt metrical constraints. This technical precision allows his poetry to maintain lyrical clarity while carrying a heavy moral weight. His metaphors are often multilayered, shifting between the spiritual and the tangible, the cosmic and the personal, lending his work a rare depth that invites repeated readings.

Whether readers interpret the "invisible thread" as God, conscience, or love, Kim's poetry remains open enough to speak across spiritual boundaries. His poetic voice is marked by vivid metaphor, musical balance, and moral urgency. In a fractured world, Kim's work reminds us that the poetic word can be an act of healing.

Preface

WATCHING THE NEWS ON TV these days fills me with dread. Scenes of horrific destruction in war-torn countries, extreme weather events such as heavy snow, heatwaves, and devastating floods caused by climate change, and frequent reports of heinous crimes fill the broadcasts.

Many people, while watching such news, feel anxiety and fear, yet remain indifferent and disengaged, absorbed in their own lives as passive bystanders. Some politicians tend to be more concerned with their own fame and political gains than with sincerely dedicating themselves to solving these pressing issues.

I wrote this collection of poems to reflect on these global crises and to urge people around the world to join in reflection and action, using the image of tears, rich in symbolic meaning.

To effectively achieve this purpose, I plan to publish translated editions in English, French, Spanish, and other languages across various countries.

For a peaceful, beautiful, and happy Earth, I hope that people everywhere will come together in prayer and cooperation.

June 1, 2025 Wansoo Kim

Part 1: Poverty, Wars and Politics

FOR WHOM DOES THE BELL RING?

For over a year, day and night,
Bombs have rained down like seeds of death
Across the skies of Russia and Ukraine.

Among the rubble of collapsed apartments,
The staggering footsteps of refugees down the desolate roads.
In the ruins of a hospital, bloodied scalpels lie still,
A white coat sowing cries into the empty air.

In the hushed classrooms of gutted schools,
Tiny shoulders of children whose eyes have lost their light.
The war's swelling clouds grow darker by the day,
Spreading beyond Europe, blanketing the world.

Where life splinters beneath the roar of missiles,
Trembling breaths of the bleeding citizens rise skyward.
No longer fragrant petals—only limp, silent flowers.

I do not know for whom the bell tolls—
But the bells of war tear through all our hearts.

THE SILENT GODS

At dawn on the Sabbath, thousands of shells
Tear through the quiet night sky,
Thunderous red rain falls down on Israel's land,
An old Israeli man opens his Bible and weeps.

Storm clouds carrying tempests gather
Over a land engulfed in wrath.
Like flocks of migratory birds, bombers swoop,
Missiles plunge toward Palestine like meteors,
And Israel's boiling blood turns into blazing flames,
Swallowing the ancient land.
A Palestinian girl stands dazed before her shattered home.

Flames devour the desert, buildings collapse,
Instead of angelic trumpets, cries fill the air.
Fragile lives wither like flower petals,
The names of gods scatter as black ash,
The sky is stained crimson, the earth turns to hell.

Palestine cries out to Allah, Israel to Yahweh,
But only dry prayers flow from their empty lips.
The Bible and the Quran are stained with blood,
Where love once grew, hatred sprouts like poison weeds.

Before the human dance of swords,
High in the heavens, two gods silently close their eyes.
Do they not listen to the pain of mankind?
Or have humans themselves left the embrace of the gods?

LET US BECOME EMBERS

In the bloody war between Israel and Hamas,
Hostages are caught in hidden snares,
Like birds with broken wings,
Amid gunfire and explosions,
Their hearts tighten, wrapped in darkness.

The groans of hostages cover the earth,
And even the sky sobs, soaked in silent weeping.
In the darkness of suffocating explosions,
How long must the crushed blades of trembling souls
Be trampled underfoot?

In the deep shadow, cries echo,
Spreading across the world, brushing past our ears.
With what radiant light and seething heart
Can we break the endless chains of darkness?

How much longer trapped in the muddy mire of numbers,
Gazing at the sky with cold eyes?
In the silent night, a scream that shreds the ears
Spreads across the sky bruised with blood.

Let us engrave in our hearts
That every flower blooming on this earth
Holds the breath of life we should protect.
And grant that we may become
Embers burning together in the darkness.

POETS, LET US RISE TOGETHER

Poets,
Let us now raise a flag with the language of peace.
Though we cannot silence the gunfire,
We can breathe in warm breaths, gentle winds
Into this land.

Poets,
Let us kindle the fire of love together.
Though we cannot make laws that forbid war,
We can plant warm poems
That spring like hot springs in frozen hearts.

Poets,
Let us lift the lantern of wisdom.
Though we cannot completely hush evil's whisper,
We can send poems to shine the path with a merciful light,
Which will not be swept away
By the flames of revenge.

Poets,
Let us hesitate no longer.
Even now,
Youth fall to bullets,
Refugees wander like stars that have lost their way,
And orphans' tears quietly seep into the ruins.
Now is the time for poetry to speak.

CRY FOR NORTH KOREA 2

A single bloodline, deeply rooted,
The northern land
Has sunk for seventy years in rivers dark and
Beyond closed iron gates,
Longing hands are cut.

In the North,
Hunched backs carry bricks and stones,
Empty bowls grasped by frozen hands
Cast lives onto the Tumen's ice.
In the South, to hide the belly's trace,
Money pours out at pharmacy or hospital doors.
In the same blood's flowing waves,
Can waves be so far apart?

Last summer, the sky wept tears
That flooded even homes away.
Among fallen houses,
Where shadows of death fall hard,
Is there no warm hand to reach?
A heart-wrenching pain wraps all over.

People of the South, shed your tears,
Don't you hear the silent cry
Of starving brothers?
Longing still breathes—
Let us join hands and pray
For children's laughter to bloom
In North and South alike.

CRY FOR SOUTH KOREA 2

O land of the North,
Seventy years ago, flames of vengeance rose—
A rain of shells poured down,
Soaking the southern soil in blood.
Is that stain not still spreading beneath your eyelids?

We sent you sacks of rice,
Yet the flame, like a burning tongue, would not die.
Even the green fields of the South—
Must they be buried in ash?
Do their hearts still burn?

Behind the missile's flash and nuclear glare,
You hide your tear-soaked pillow each night.
Before the people you called your foes,
Has your chest not grown heavier?

As the years pass,
The cries of the starving grow deeper still.
Yet your leader—
How long will he shut his eyes
To the hunger masked behind glittering slogans?

O leader of the North,
If your heart still stirs,
Bring forth the dusty smile of childhood
And reveal the soul stained with tears.

BREATH BENEATH THE SILENCE

Like a bear, China
Claims Taiwan as part of its own flesh,
Growling threats time and again.
But Taiwan, like a rabbit,
Stomps hard upon its own ground,
Eyes wide open,
Refusing to smooth its bristled back.

Watching closely, the U.S.
Sends warships to Taiwan's coast
To block China's ragged breath.
China, with fleets of ships and planes,
Narrows the ocean's fence,
Unleashing threats like crashing waves.

China and the U.S.
Stand with no space between,
Backs arched like drawn bows.
Taiwan, eyes burning red,
Peers beneath China's looming shadow,
Ears pricked
At every word exchanged.

The night sky is filled with glittering stars,
The sea remains tranquil through the night,
Yet like waves concealed beneath the calm,
Taiwan stays awake all night, preparing for the storm.

EARTHQUAKE IN AFGHANISTAN

In a single moment
An entire village turned into a graveyard—
In that hellish place,
Those clinging to life
Cry out in cracked voices
From the darkness between collapsed walls.

The whole world,
With eyes caught by the flames
Of Israel and Palestine,
Shuts its eyes and ears
To Afghanistan's fallen mounds of earth.

Pale faces,
Flinch at even the touch of wind on their skin.
In the unlit dark, with open eyes,
They embrace the night.
Though their chests curl inward,
No more tears will come.

Stars scattered in the sky
Quietly scan the ashes below,
Blinking with breath-like light,
Whispering that the fragile breath
May bloom again from broken hearts.

BEYOND BROKEN PROMISES

Whenever I think of you,
A black hook sinks deep in my chest.
Ash-gray waves rush in,
And I wanted to exhale a deeply bitter wind,
Carried by ragged breaths.

Even in the shadow of a crumpled life,
Intoxicated by your sweet whisper,
I floated upon silky waves
And soaked into a field of dazzling poisonous flowers.

Your shining touch—
Like a magical spell, I held tight.
I, who wanted to easily tear down
The towering wall,
Was a foolish dreamer.

Now, I will open my eyes,
Face the hidden light,
And with tender eyes bearing wounds,
I will find my way.

No longer leaning on faded letters,
Following the compass of my heart,
I will walk toward the path that wipes away tears.
A single spark alive in my chest will breathe.

THE RIVER OF WAITING

Even when I'm irritated or weary,
I will lay down the sharp stones aimed at you
And hide the fire-lit or ice-cold glint in my eyes.

Even beneath the dust of all the passing time,
I won't turn away or give you my back—
I'll quietly wait like a mother by the window.

Even when you stir up clouds of dust,
I'll soothe your back instead of striking with thorns,
Believing your roots still breathe below.

So that petal-like smiles may bloom on every face,
I'll listen to the echoes of mingled voices in the square,
And when you knock on hardened walls,
I'll walk with you until warm sweat beads on your brow.

In the tangle of clashing cries,
I'll light a small candle to guard the breath of truth,
And sing a song that binds neighbors,
Shoulder to shoulder, into one,
And pray like a river that never ceases to flow.

A PRAYER FOR LEADERS

O Heaven above,
Those who once plowed the fields of the lowly
And shed honest sweat,
Now plant their flags on the people's tears
And sit atop the peak of power.

Ah, if even a faint flame
Still burns within their hearts,
Recalling the scent of sweat
That once drenched their backs,
Let them gently take those frozen hands
In the alleys where sunlight never reaches.

In the heavy fog scattered by hollow words,
Let the night of those who sobbed pass away,
And let a dawn come
When warm sunlight spreads across every yard.

Let the embers within their hearts never fade.
Let them bow their heads as if kneeling in grass,
Listening to the voices of parched lips,
Placing their hands on torn skin, and weeping together.

O Heaven above,
Let those who lead this land become your wind,
Sowing warm seeds into the barren earth,
And tending green fields
Where children's songs fill every alley.

Part 2: Environment Pollution

SADNESS OF THE MOON

A woman draped
In a silver wave-like robe,
Silently gliding through the darkness.

Does she wander this land,
With her deep eyes
Searching for a love long lost?

Above the coldly glimmering signs
And the dazzling city lights,

On the tear-streaked face
Of the woman bereft of her light,
A gentle sob lingers,
And the wind, with a heart-wrenching sorrow,
Calls out her name.

Yet the woman,
In the deep blue darkness,
Embraces this world once more
With the light of her wistful longing.

TEARS OF THE SEA

The sea sobs.
Black oil and decayed wastewater
Choke birds with stilled wings,
And fish that have lost their breath.
Swarming piles of garbage
Trample the sea's naked flesh.

The sea rides on rough waves,
And in the suffocating stench,
It cries out like a dying breath—
"Black water scales are spreading all over my body,
My once-blue breath has grown thin, about to break."

Humans pass the sea like the wind,
But the sea never stops its tears,
Sending letters written in white foam
To the shoreline every single day.

"If I stop breathing,
Your dreams too
Will scatter like broken seashells.
Only when fish dance in my arms
Will your future breathe again."

SEA MONSTERS

Brilliant monsters
Swarm in groups,
Capsize fishing boats,
Or overrun fish farms.

When the typhoon rages,
Colossal beings surge like mountains,
Blanketing the sea.

Fishermen, with sighs filled with despair,
Dig into its belly,
Shedding tears of anger.

Most of the colorful monsters
Are hems of garments that dance upon the waves,
Like altars cloaked in shining shells,

The women who drift on the tides of passing trends
May never know
Their clothes trample fishermen's lives
And the breath of the sea.

Within the garments they wear
Hides microplastic, quiet as breath,
Lingering for generations—
A hidden seed of death.

FUKUSHIMA'S CONTAMINATED WATER

Fukushima, the sea bearing deep wounds
Inside the silent heart of the nuclear plant,
Invisible seeds flow out,
Riding the lifeline of our blue planet,
And seep even into children's dreams.

Among the words spilled from entangled lips,
Shattered fragments scatter in the waves,
Wandering through twisted alleys,
Empty eyes sway with murky currents.

The fishermen's eyes are wet with salty tears,
And the cries spreading to the sky echo unanswered.
Oars misaligned by divided winds now rest still,
Beneath the rotting nets,
The sea sways like a ship that has lost its way.

From the wellspring deep in pain's core,
Masked currents flow,
Black waves smother the breath of the sea.
Layers of darkness,
Hoping to scatter on the breeze,
With eyes shut, the sea quietly holds its breath.

INTRUDER IN THE WIND

The bomber of the wind
Frequently crosses the Chinese border
And showers fine dust, dressed in bacteria or viruses,
Like tear gas
Across the Korean Peninsula.

The invader hidden behind each breath
Seeps into every shadow on the street,
Covering both young breaths and aged pulses alike,
Secretly embracing the lungs,
Penetrating deep into the veins.

The dust flowing along the veins
Moves far inside the body,
Scattering invisible seeds of disease.

Even when we try to shield our breath,
The hidden dust grows more fierce,
Burrowing into the deepest nest of life within.
It seems small and fragile,
But its whisper spreads like a poison that gnaws at the bone.

How can we get rid of that dark shadow of his?
We cry out to the heavens but the air scatters only excuses.
Gasping for breath,
We search for faint answers like ashes drifting into the wind.
When will the sky's clear light descend into our hearts?

A SONG DEDICATED TO THE SPRING WIND

Blow, O spring wind,
I long for your mysterious breath of love
That brings buds and blossoms
To the dry branches.

Beneath the black shadow bearing death,
Come into the veins of my shrunken heart,
Melt away the remnants hidden deep in the darkness,
And unfold the buds and blossoms of hopeful dreams.

Blow, O spring wind,
Please seize the dark shadow of COVID
And hurl it
Beyond the edge of the sky.

With unmasked faces,
Hand in hand with friends,
We want to walk along your fragrant flower path,
And let a spring of laughter fully blossom,
Sharing the memories of the COVID war
Like fairy tales.

INVERTED SEASONS

On a late autumn morning,
As I walk through the park,
A red rose, out of season,
Greets me with a smile.

In the Piedmont region of Italy,
Summer showers fall,
Suddenly turning into a heavy snowfall.

As days go by,
The seasons rage like beasts unbridled,
Firing lightning without warning,
Unleashing blizzards that howl
Their lament.

But humans,
Turn away from glaciers melting in pain,
Piling trash beneath the lights,
Waving gray flags high,
Setting black flowers afloat on the waves.

The clock of disaster in the sky
Looks at the earth with pitying eyes,
Its hands flow like sand toward the end.
Is there still a faint ray of light?
Listen closely to the whispering wind.

IN THE MAZE OF FOG

In the sea of pouring information,
Truth drifts in silence like a lonely island.
Falsehoods and deepfakes, like full-bloomed flowers,
Dance like vipers draped in silk patterns.
We, searching for hidden light,
Drift through the fog like a ship without a compass.

In the storm of provocative videos and thumbnails,
We chase shadows in the mirror
And shatter our lives into the eyes of others.
Within the vast maze woven by algorithms,
No one dares to open the silent eyes of conscience.

A phone rings, then a strange chord spreads,
And a honey-coated trap slowly approaches.
A whirlwind of desire surges in an instant,
But a blade-like will severs its tether.

In the darkness where truth and illusion intertwine,
Countless people chase after sparkling bubbles
And surrender themselves to dreams vanishing like air.

The path we turned away from is brushed by dry winds,
Yet at its end, the breeze reveals a quiet face,
Blooming like a clear breath
From between mossy stones in the forest's deep heart.
We pass through a road where ghostly scents scatter,
Gently following the breath of starlight

THE DIGITAL SEA

Digital fragments
Floating on the waves of the internet.

Amid the stench of rotting trash,
The seawater grows more foul day by day.

Gales, thick with deceitful dust,
Churn the sea without rest,
And even the roots of once-green trees are shaken.

As trash mountains rise up
In the digital sea,
Flowers of temptation bloom
Like colorful poisonous mushrooms.

Those entranced by the alluring fragrance of flowers
Find their gaze dimming
And their words vanish like the wind
Without even realizing.

MASKS OF LIES

The words flowing from their mouths
Are sweet like lollipops,
But foxes harboring poison laugh,
Disguised in sheep's wool.

Into the hearts of children flying blue kites
Falls betrayal, cold as rain.

Lonely shadows wearing golden crowns before mirrors
Smile into the void.

With the sunbeam smile
Of a baby's face filled with the scent of milk,
Clear away the fog of hypocrisy tangled like a spiderweb.

With the hot tears
Flowing down calloused hands,
Open the heart's door, sealed like a rusted lock.

Plant a tree of justice bearing time's rings
Instead of concrete walls,
And with the unemployed man
Sitting in front of the corner store at the alley's end,
The old man with silver hair fluttering,
And the child in a wheelchair,
Tend the wildflower-covered hill,
With thick drops of sweat.

Part 3: Confusion of Values

LIGHT BLOOMING IN THE DARKNESS

In the spotlight, a golden ring hung around the neck,
A splendid flag raised at the edge of a cliff,
Cheers soar high, like the wind.

Breath held, I ran a long, weary road,
The heart pounded like a drum,
But an empty chair quietly weighed on the soul.

Some pave the path with sweat and tears,
While others set themselves ablaze,
Burying a star of hope within the darkness of the world.

Like a shadow creeping into light,
Beneath the dazzling facade,
In search of the hidden light, we wander.

Like a flower that blooms after a harsh winter,
Like a star that shines in the darkness,
To kindle a single spark within us—
That warmth is the gentle flame
That blooms in the silence.

MASTER OF LIFE

Today again, following the current of time,
The boat of life
Sails upon storm-tossed seas of the world.

At times, chasing a yearning that blazes like fire,
At times, pursuing dreams warm as sunlight,
At times, in a stillness veiled in fog,
One rows with trembling hands, burdened and slow.

Like a jar always thirsty,
The drops that overflow from another's cup
Stir ripples of envy within the heart.

When a sudden whirlwind strikes
And shadows like black beasts stain the soul,
A single starlight deep within me whispers:

"Like the deep and silent night sky,
Embrace stillness even in the midst of chaos.
That light shining through your darkness
Is an invisible thread binding us together.

Follow that light—
Raise the sail of hope upon gentle waves,
And open your own course.

The starlight will embrace your weary boat
And guide you, like a compass, to a harbor of rest."

LIGHTLESS EYES

Parent 1: I am a lawyer. You must guide the students properly.
If any unjust incident occurs, I will sue you.

Parent 2: How do you care for kids?
Do you treat my child like a mentally ill patient?
Do you know how much my child is struggling?

A Teacher's Diary: Phone calls and texts from parents
Constrict my throat each day.
Every night, their echoing voices pierce my heart with needles.
My pillow is soaked in endless tears,
And I sink deeper into the dark.
Life feels unbearable;
I want to break free from days bound by iron chains.

A student: Lately, the teacher often seems sad.
The teacher's eyes look like a light-lost moon.

Citizen 1: These days, some parents
Have eyes without a compass.
Do they see teachers as just disposable objects?
The once proud nation
Now remains a sentence buried in dusty bookmarks.

Citizen 2: The government must speak:
Children's dreams bloom in a teacher's gaze,
And when cold stares turn into warm breaths,
Laughter will once again bloom in every classroom.

THE SHADOW THAT CREPT INTO THE CLASSROOM

Darkness seeps into a sunlit classroom.
The devil's hand dances across the keyboard,
Crushing pure, innocent hearts.

Children bruised deep within
By silent pain or nameless fear
Sob beneath their blankets, haunted by nightly nightmares.

Famous sports stars or trot singers
Falter at the shadow of a memory from their youth.
Their once dazzling fame
Falls like a shooting star and disappears into darkness.

The famous politician who stood atop the tower
Wavers from a single spark of buried childhood violence,
Bricks piled high crumble into ash,
And dazzling light vanishes into thin smoke.

The violence of school days
Is a tear-stained scar
Carved deep into the tree of memory.

When a single delicate thread mends a wound,
And a small light begins to glow,
Spring returns
In the eyes of the children.

TREES OF THE SOUL

Like a red flower blooming in the family garden,
As gripping pain and cold sweat spread across the chest,
When the cry of new life bursts forth,
Joy and tears bloom together.

These days, many hesitate to embrace a fragile breath.
In empty wallets and the weight of heavy sighs,
Under icy stares at the workplace,
And crushed by a baby crying every night,
They feel a new beginning like a shadow cast on their backs.

Yet in the eyes of a grandchild with an angelic smile,
Sunlight that brightens the world shines through.
Even at the end of a weary, difficult day,
That gaze alone melts the heart.

A tree standing in the storm
Must endure both wounds and pain to grow.
Without the nourishment of sweat and tears,
Flowers and fruit cannot be colored with joy.

Childbirth is a journey of rowing endlessly over waves,
Cradling a gift from heaven
Planted in the soil.
A tiny seed becomes a forest,
And within it, we become trees of the soul,
Embracing one another, breathing as one.

CHRISTMAS EVE 2

Beneath the glittering tree,
Puppets dressed in red
Shake their bells, eyes fixed on wallets.

Under the neon light,
Motels with crimson lips open
Swallow wandering youth.

At a subway station swept by cold wind,
Passersby's hurried steps and Salvation Army bells
Sidestep the beggar's empty hands.

In the tavern,
Amid the clinking of drunken glasses,
A photo of Jesus lies face down beneath an empty glass.

In the back alley club,
Men and women, intoxicated by the lights and music,
Surrender their bodies to the beat,
Their eyes submerged in the haze of alcohol.

Heavy snow falls from the frozen sky,
Covering tear stains
On the street corner in white.

In churches, warm carols echo—
A single beam of light in the dark.

REST IN PEACE

When someone passes,
Many offer a warm smile.

Countless whispers
Rise as a gentle breeze
Toward the sky where a star has just set.

People tighten their black collars
With tear-filled eyes,
Embracing grief like the bark of an old tree.

"By now, they must have stepped
Into a land where flowers bloom beyond."

The words flowing from honeyed lips—
Can they knock, ever so softly,
On heaven's distant window between the stars?

Soft comfort melts into the air,
Too light to shake the night sky—
Only heavy silence returns.

As time layers over a handful of earth,
Tears seep into the ground,
And waiting for the day we meet again,
They hold the departed's smile in their hearts.

A PUPPY AND A BEGGAR

A young woman walking with her puppy
Sends a loving smile
To the puppy with sparkling eyes,
And gently feeds it frequently.

Nearby,
A beggar with tangled hair and a worn-out coat,
And lets his gaze quietly rest on the dog,
Wrapping his arms around his hungry belly.

Passing the beggar with swift steps
As if they had seen a worm,
People offer a bright smile
To the dog.

To the people with cheerful eyes
The dog had been wagging its tail,
But it flinches, turns to the beggar,
And barks at him.

The beggar, who had gazed warmly at the dog,
Feels frozen stares brush his nape like a cold wind,
Swallows something burning inside,
And lowers his head to the ground.

A DIALOGUE BETWEEN A MOTHER AND DAUGHTER

I water the dream trees of my husband and children
With the waters of love and prayer,
Gazing at their blossoms and fruit,
Savoring the sweetness in my heart—
These are life's most radiant moments.
So why won't you marry?

In a world of wind and rain,
Even tending my own dream tree wears me out.
To be caught in the harness of marriage,
Forsaking my dreams,
Just to water his and the children's
With tears? I can't do that.

Walking alone may be free and unburdened at times,
But it can be lonely and difficult
To climb that mountain alone.
Wouldn't it be better to climb it with a partner
Looking up at the same star,
Hand in hand, encouraging each other with love?

Please don't hurry.
I will draw more water from the well of my heart.

THE TRAGEDY OF POWER

To many politicians,
Power gleams like a beckoning crown,
Sparkling under dazzling spotlights.

To seize it,
They shatter the net of law and the mirror of morality,
Summoning black winds in their wake,
And at times, end up behind iron bars.

Yet just once
They sink their teeth into that sweet fruit,
Bound by invisible chains,
Wandering endlessly through a muddy maze.

Even as mocking winds strike their torn faces,
The electric taste still clings to their tongues,
And they pursue its scent to their final breath.

But beneath a night sky heavy with storm clouds,
Someone plants a handful of embers,
Stepping away from the swirling crimson blaze,
Raising a flag high at the edge of the cliff,
Walking toward the path of light.

INVISIBLE PRISON

After Adam and Eve
Tasted the forbidden fruit,
Their hearts, once like clear stream water, grew murky,
And calculator lights flashed in their eyes.

When asked why they ate the fruit,
They did not bow their heads,
But strung together
Words like seashells.

Beyond the screen, countless windows
Wear golden masks and issue commands.

Many are caught
In a shimmering tangle of threads.
With their guiding star lost,
They flounder among numbers,
Wings that once dreamed of the blue sky
Now fold against invisible walls.

FLOWERS BLOOMING THROUGH SHARING

Many people
Turn their thoughts and steps
Toward the golden fruit before their eyes.

But blessings,
The more you reach for them,
Scatter like mist over water.

The sky first
Pours out light and rain,
Smiling at the flowers in silence.

In every cloudy pause of daily life,
Like sunlight pouring through the window,
Offer the warmth that seeps into you—
With a quiet gift from dawn.

Rather than striving to clutch,
On the emptied palm
The world lays fragrant flowers
And ripening fruit.

Blessings become dawn mist,
Brushing near like a breath,
Spreading songs resting on the leaves,
And letting green life
Sprout through barren cracks.

Part 4: God and Humans

THE QUEER FESTIVAL IN KOREA

In the square where the parade's waves ripple
Upon the tides of music,
Long-held silence, hidden beneath radiant masks
And garments of vibrant hues, bursts forth as dance.
On bright streets drenched in countless gazes,
They sketch the sky with the movements of freedom.

A weeping young man, calling out the unspoken name,
Men embracing, women kissing—
Hold passersby in silent awe.

Teenagers, caught between strange excitement and fear,
Gleam with curious eyes.
Middle-aged swallow uneasy breaths, turning away.
While some citizens join the dance,
Raising voices of concern.

In the plaza mixed with cheers and sighs, laughter and tears,
Everyone's heart is touched by fleeting glances.

Beneath the rainbow-colored flag,
Tears of light and shadow flow over dancing souls.
Rain falls from the sky like a heartfelt prayer,
Soaking the parched, cracked earth as if by healing hands,
And it sprouts new shoots.

THE FRUIT OF THE KNOWLEDGE OF GOOD AND EVIL

On that day filled with sweet fragrance of the forbidden fruit,
Adam blamed Eve, and Eve blamed the serpent
For eating its fruit.

On the day children fail the test,
They blame their parents,
And parents blame their ancestors,
For their poor performance in studies,

On the day workers were kicked out of their job,
They blame employers,
And the people blame the government.

Today, many people believe
That Adam and Eve ate the fruit
Because God created the tree of knowledge.

To those who love to blame others,
There is one who strokes their backs with rough hands,
Lighting a candle by the window—
That love embraces every breath and waits.

Facing a stranger's eyes in the mirror,
Like pulling out thorns buried deep in the flesh,
The barefoot path wet with dust and dirt
Will become the rain that wakes sleeping flowers.

THE TOWER OF BABEL

Like those who once built the Tower of Babel long ago,
People today build their own towers of glass.

Deep within their hearts,
Golden flames rise,
And the flag of honor stirs the wind.
They struggle without rest, shedding blood and sweat,
To engrave their names
Like the brightest star in the night sky.

They treat the breath of unreachable heights
As cold starlight,
Without even a glance,
Letting its unknown movement
Drift past like the strange, distant sound of the wind.

Some, as their towers grow taller,
Seek to rise above many shadows;
Others dream of becoming the heart of the world,
To shake the lifeblood of all living things.

Beneath the starlight, atop the tower they built,
A sob seeps through the fractured seams
And quietly disperses into the night sky.
Yet they still cover their ears to the murmuring,
Insisting on their own path, walking on alone.

STARS IN THE DARKNESS

Are Black people
Stars born in the midnight wilderness?
Fragments of light
That never fade in the dark?
Or are they beings trapped in shadows,
Struck by God's arrows of wrath?

Their light is not a curse—
It is another sun awakening the world.

Just as each petal holds its own color,
Just as forest creatures sing with their own cries,
Stories lived along the grain of time
Like patterns woven by countless hands,
Bloom diverse scents and light,
Coloring the world more deeply and richly.

Do not weigh
Someone's breath
By the color of their shell.

Every color
Is a hidden treasure of the rainbow,
Blooming from the deep cracks of darkness.
Raindrops and sunlight meet,
A mysterious bridge hung across the sky—
Its light is a song of hope
Settling on the wounds of the world.

LIGHT FALLING ON WOUNDS

The whole earth
Is crying out
With the pus of its split wounds.

Minarets of Islam and crosses of churches,
Black skin and blue eyes,
Sparks in seething hearts
Of those who raise different flags
Are spreading like lightning across the earth.

Amid burning words and sharp gazes,
The weary hold their collapsing knees
And gaze at a sky that offers no reply.

To give them a light that never fades
And a dawn that will surely come,
The one who endured spittle and stones
Whispers:

"Daily awaken the seeds of love
That sleep deep within your hearts.
Like spring rain nurturing life in barren soil,
As you look into each other's eyes and join hands
Embracing the scars of pain with a warm smile,
The forests of this land will gradually grow lush."

THE CHOICE OF PATHS

Many people
Flock like migratory birds
To the road glittering with golden shells,
That looks so convincing to the eye.

But those who fail to catch them
Collapse with suffocating hearts and misted eyes,
Recalling the countless paths they once ignored
And the time they lost,
Letting out dry sighs.

The breath of ancient wisdom whispers:
Pass beyond the dazzling trap like glass beads,
And listen closely to the breath of the forest path
Where shards of sunlight pour down.
That path offers, instead of sparkling stones,
The chirping of birds
And the song of the wind.
There, lost souls
Will find a tiny starlight.

Even if life's steps bend
And thorny bushes tangle your way,
Follow the hidden ember burning inside your heart.
At the end of that path, beyond the dense shadows,
New wings will sprout, and a bright world will unfold.
When trapped and wandering in darkness,
An echo rising from the depths will light a single path.

A SONG HEARD IN THE DARKNESS

The 21st century, a civilization of iron and fire,
Sways like a murky fog as in primordial darkness.

On every brow of the Earth,
Volcanoes of war erupt with fire,
Rivers overflow, swallowing fields whole,
The parched land weeps with cracked lips,
Unseen shadows
Spread through the breath of cities.

Days gripped by fear,
Like sharp gears of unrest,
Turn endlessly on this earth—
How can we bear fruit
And sing our songs?
Who will pierce this darkness
And call forth the dawn?

From the silence of the beginning,
A breath that called the first light is heard:
"I dwell in every step you take,
Watching always with wakeful eyes.
Do not weep for the darkness yet to come;
Wounds will bloom into flowers someday."

Even at midnight, the stars remain awake,
And a single seed fallen from a cliff
Becomes a forest, breathing life.

THE ETERNAL LIGHTHOUSE

He embraced the enemy who killed his two sons,
At times swallowing the rising tears,
At times, when children's laughter brushed by in the wind,
Clutching his heart, crossing nights of wailing,
He let blood-red prayers seep into the calluses of a new son.

Turning his back on the altar of Japanese rule,
Though imprisoned behind iron bars in the dark,
A single teardrop that fell to the ground
Shone all the brighter like starlight in the night.

"O fierce wind that strikes me,
Try to break me with your blade of cold,
From the crimson blood stained on the blade's tip,
You will witness the miracle of sacred love."

Until the last day his breath faded away,
He blew warmth into the wounds of the hungry,
Lived without extinguishing the flame through the dark dawns,
And became a light that never dies in raging waves.
Even now, it lights up the night of this land.

This poem is inspired by the true story of pastor Yang-won Son, who forgave the man who murdered his two sons and adopted him as his own. He was imprisoned for refusing to bow to Japanese shrines during the occupation and was later martyred during the Korean War, choosing to remain with the patients he served.

ALBERT SCHWEITZER OF THE EAST

Wherever he went throughout his life,
He touched the oozing wounds of the sick,
With fingertips steeped in the scent of earth,
He etched warmth into their barren hearts.

To a passing beggar,
He offered his pay envelope, worn with use,
And under the lights of the operating room,
He stayed up all night, hands clasped,
Guarding a patient's breath.

During the Korean War, he fled south,
Yet could never let go of his wife left behind in the North.
He lived alone his whole life,
Often casting tearful eyes toward the northern sky.

He wore his medical gown until it frayed,
While two suits in the closet slept beneath layers of dust.
They once called him a fool,
But one day, before his empty chair in a desolate room,
They bowed their heads with folded hands.

Dr. Kiryeo Jang was a respected Christian physician, the founder of Busan Gospel Hospital, and the creator of the Blue Cross Medical Insurance Association. He is renowned for his life of humble poverty and service and is known by nicknames such as "the foolish doctor," "Korea's Schweitzer," and "the little Jesus."

THE ET-LIKE GRANDPA

In his youth, in a car accident,
His whole body caught fire,
Thirty times he crossed the blade's precipice,
With hot, flowing tears of prayer,
Reborn with the face of an alien.

His face disfigured, hair planted for eyebrows,
Eyelids and lips made from different skin,
And a prosthetic eye implanted in his right eye.

He ultimately shook off the abyss of despair,
Cradling one ember in his heart, keeping it from dying,
Even in the pitch-black, he held stars in his eyes.
Passing barefoot through cold stares and thorny paths,
He held children's hands and built classrooms,
On poster-filled streets, he burned his voice.

His flame-like life, burning through his whole body,
Even at the tip of a crayon in a small hand,
Even in deep night's soliloquies,
It ignites the fire
That says one can live.

Mr. Gyucheol Chae engaged in various social activities through the Rose Association assisting epilepsy patients and the Sorok Island Volunteer Corps aiding Hansen's disease patients. And Additionally he founded the Dumilli Nature School for children's education.

LOVE THAT KEEPS THE EMBER ALIVE

The word love
Wears all kinds of shining clothes
And dances on the screen,
But by a dark window at the street's end,
Empty eyes endure the day.

On the land of Africa,
Children clutching their bellies cry,
And under the skies of Israel and Palestine,
Red smoke and gunfire
Drive people into darkness.

Is love sitting beside the sick,
A hand wiping sweat from their brow?
Or a heart that quietly,
Without words, soaks in their tears?

Beside the lost,
Lighting a small lamp,
In the trembling glow,
Feeling out the path of hope,
And standing against the cold wind—

When we hand over a warm bowl of soup,
Gently hold a dry hand,
Listen to the lonely one's story,
Love quietly takes root
And will become someone's ember.

A SEED

A storehouse of life
Filled with endless dreams.

Inside the hard shell,
A blueprint for a forest lies hidden.
It prepares for the season planted by the sky—
Who could ever guess?

A seed waits for years in the dark soil,
But with the blessing of sunlight and rain,
It struggles to take root
In the narrow crevices of rocks,
And then, it emerges into the world, lifting its head.

How did the Designer of all things
Place hidden light
In the deep darkness of a tiny seed
And breathe into it a life as strong as steel?

Do not let me be bound
By the traces of my past and present.
Let me trust the first step
Of the new life He has planted in me,
And each day, like spring's first breeze,
Breathe a warm breath into the tender sprout.

A CRY FOR THE EARTH

Oh, Keeper of the Stars,
In Ukraine and Palestine,
Beneath skies torn by flames,
Echoes of screams seep into the air.

Sipping muddy water in hunger,
The gaze of a parched child in Africa
Shatters the heart like glass.

The ocean, choked by a black breath,
Heaves with the wail of a whale,
And a polar bear with nowhere to go
Sways, clinging to the edge of a drifting ice floe.

Those lost in the fog of greed,
Holding torches of power,
Deafen themselves to the cries of a ruptured earth
And clash blades beneath banners, sharing only spoils.
Thus, humanity hurls itself into the pit of darkness.

Oh, Keeper of the Stars,
Let bloodstained soil breathe once more,
And on this land steeped in despair,
Kindle a single star of hope,
That by its light, we may walk into a world of smiles.

THE ANGEL OF SLEEP

As the morning sun rises high,
And sends forth radiant beams,
My eyes light up with a smile,
Gently saying farewell
To the fairy of dreams who stayed through the night.

At night, as I lie in bed,
My eyes part ways with light,
Welcoming the wandering dark—
Sleep's angel lands with gentle wings.

This angel softens every muscle,
Like gentle waves it soothes,
Letting peace seep deeply in
To the heart's innermost place,
Melting gently into a land of dreams,
Spreading like a whisper of starlight,
Softly covering the tender, hidden wounds.

Each night, the angel of sleep
Gently touches the hour with the moon's breath,
Restoring body and soul—
A quiet starlight sent from the heart of the universe.

After nights of tossing, eyes wide open,
The moment I meet the fresh morning light,
To the gift softly passed by the dark
I offer a warm breath.

THE MEANING OF A FART

It blows a trumpet
Many times a day, in a variety of sounds.

It usually lets out a bold "toot-toot"
Freely when no one is around,
But near a beloved partner
Or in a cautious gathering,
It hesitates to perform willingly.

When both body and mind feel bright and clear,
It bursts out with a lively, joyful "toot-toot",
Drifting away like a clear and gentle breath.

When under heavy stress
Or when the belly is restless,
It plays its instrument more often than usual,
Accompanied by a low "squeak"
And an unpleasant scent.

After intestinal surgery,
With the instrument's first sound,
Life dances beyond the pain
Of the stitched wound.

A warm smile gently spreads across the work of the One
Who gifted us a small instrument,
So we might sense the body's whispers
Through the pitch and smell of sound.

THE WATER POUCH INSIDE MY BODY

A whispering compass, a guide for the water's path,
A tiny pouch hidden beneath the skin,
Always measuring the rise and fall of water.

Each time the water slowly rises,
My swollen lower belly
Sends a signal softly.

Even in the deep valley of sleep,
It works without rest,
Seeping between breaths,
Guarding the slender stream.

Along unseen crevices,
Waves slip between capillaries,
Gathering like dewdrops, then flowing again,
Slowly filling the inside of me.

At night these days, like a faint current,
A slight tremble touches my nerves,
And the sleeping skin awakens.

When a gentle ripple
Lets a flow like spring water leak out,
A single leaf upon the water
Quietly finds its place.

SALIVARY GLAND

When delicious food approaches,
A clear wave fills the mouth,
Sending tiny signals through the body,
Whispering of hunger.

In front of the plate of meat,
A dog drools,
Its paws bouncing with excitement,
Its tail joyfully dancing.

The gentle spring within the mouth
Sends food gliding down like a slide,
Kindles a spark inside the body to awaken vitality,
Pushes back unseen foes,
Lays a dewdrop-like breath upon wounds,
And seeps out quietly whenever it is needed.

A spring gently hidden beneath the tongue's hollow
Is a softly resting smile.
Its warmth glows with radiant light.

As time flows and the wax of years builds,
When dryness settles in the mouth,
A lonely breeze passes through,
And this small gift
Returns like a gentle wave,
Spreading warmth across the cracked tip of the tongue.

www.ingramcontent.com/pod-product-compliance
Lightning Source LLC
LaVergne TN
LVHW020657100826
845148LV00012B/2539

* 9 7 9 8 3 8 5 2 7 3 2 7 0 *

"Wansoo Kim's poetry collection, *Exclamation Mark of Tears*, explores the pain and crises of contemporary society—such as war, hunger, and environmental destruction—through vivid and sensuous metaphorical imagery. In particular, he employs exclamations, metaphors, and symbols effectively, delivering both artistic resonance and deep emotional impact to the reader. His poetry goes beyond mere denunciation or explanation, offering profound insight into reality through refined poetic language.

"This poetic language avoids a dogmatic tone, instead approaching the reader in a voice of heartfelt pleading and supplication. Especially through the speaker's earnest prayers and impassioned cries, the poems not only move the reader emotionally but also prompt ethical reflection on the world we live in.

"Kim carries on the lineage of the zealous ethical spirit found in the Hebrew prophets of the Old Testament—Isaiah, Daniel, and Jeremiah. Within the Korean context, he connects to the ethical consciousness of historical figures such as the Six Martyred Ministers, Shik Jo, Yak-Yong Jeong, and more recently, Seok-Heon Ham, Chi-Hwan Yu, Du-Jin Park, and Sang Gu. He is a poet with a distinctive prophetic voice rooted in ethical conviction.

"The prophetic self—the speaker in his poems—rebukes the unspeakable absurdities and moral perversions of modern society. His poetic indignation rises against global poverty and war, including the suffering in Africa and North Korea, and the atrocities of the Russia-Ukraine and Israel-Hamas conflicts, often driven by wicked political leaders. He fiercely denounces the environmental destruction brought about by post-Enlightenment humanism, the dehumanization caused by dazzling digital technology, the blind frenzy of humanity driven by insatiable desire, the collapse of ethical strongholds seen in school violence, the arrogance of idolizing knowledge, and the moral failings of religious elites who betray love.

"Ultimately, the poetic voice offers a path of ethical renewal and salvation to a fallen humanity. Instead of a path of division, conflict, and hatred, he proposes the path of love—for the sake of encounter. He offers examples such as Pastor Yang-Won Son, the martyr of love; Dr. Gi-Ryeo Jang, the saintly doctor; and Gyu-Cheol Chae, the tireless social activist. Finally, the poetic self becomes a fervent voice of prayer, presenting the 'seed' filled with latent potential.

"Through a tearful, heartfelt prayer of love, the poet awakens us to the choice that transcends the tragedy of separation, hatred, and strife. This is the fruit of prophetic intellect. In the twenty-first century, Wansoo Kim stands as a forerunner who has taken up the mantle of prophetic intellect in Korea."

—Bong-Gun Kim, Literary Critic, Professor Emeritus,
Catholic University of Korea